SO-AVG-891

GEORGE W. BUSH

HERÓN MÁRQUEZ

In Consultation with Martha Cosgrove, M.A. and Reading Specialist

JUST THE FACTS BIOGRAPHIES

LERNER PUBLICATIONS COMPANY / MINNEAPOLIS

With great love and admiration to my wife, Traecy, whose soaring spirit is matched only by her beauty and her sense of humor.

Martha Cosgrove has a master's degree from the University of Minnesota in secondary education, with an emphasis on developmental and remedial reading. She is licensed in 7–12 English and language arts, developmental reading, and remedial reading. She has had several works published and gives numerous state and national presentations in her areas of expertise.

Lerner Publications Company
A division of Lerner Publishing Group
241 First Avenue North
Minneapolis, MN 55401 U.S.A.

Website address: www.lernerbooks.com

Library of Congress Cataloging-in-Publication Data

Márquez, Herón.
   George W. Bush / by Herón Márquez.
     p.   cm. − (Just the facts biographies)
   Includes bibliographical references and index.
   ISBN-13: 978–0–8225–2647–6 (lib. bdg. : alk. paper)
   ISBN-10: 0–8225–2647–6 (lib. bdg. : alk. paper)
   1. Bush, George W. (George Walker), 1946− −Juvenile literature.
   2. Presidents−United States−Biography−Juvenile literature. I. Title.
II. Series.
E903.M37 2006
973.931'092−dc22   2005007883

Manufactured in the United States of America
1 2 3 4 5 6 − BP − 11 10 09 08 07 06

CONTENTS

INTRODUCTION

GEORGE WALKER BUSH WAS BORN

into a wealthy, powerful family. But this did not mean that success came easily for him. He did not do well in school. The first time he ran for political office, he lost. He also failed when he tried to run businesses. He had a drinking problem, and people often said he wasn't very smart. But on January 20, 2001, he became the forty-third president of the United States. In 2004, he was reelected to be president for another four years. He had become the most powerful man in the United States and maybe in the world.

George W. Bush won his second term as president in 2004.

His road to the White House, however, was far from smooth. Most Americans went to bed on election night, November 7, 2000, believing that they would wake up to find out who would be their new president. Instead, the election was not decided for five weeks. The vote was so close that the U.S. courts were asked to decide whether Democrat Al Gore or Republican George W. Bush had won the election. Finally, on December 12, 2000, the U.S. Supreme Court declared that George W. Bush would be the country's forty-third president.

Questions about the election results cast a cloud over Bush's presidency. Yet during his first four-year term as president, Bush led the United States through many difficult events. On September 11, 2001, terrorists attacked the World Trade Center towers in New York City and

On September 11, 2001, terrorists destroyed the 110-story World Trade Center towers in New York (right).

the Pentagon near Washington, D.C., killing almost three thousand people. Many businesses failed, and thousands of Americans lost their jobs. About two years later, the country began a bloody and unpopular war in Iraq. Many people questioned Bush's decisions as a leader. And yet, in November 2004, he was reelected with a greater number of votes than any U.S. president had ever received. But almost one-half of the country's voters were unhappy with the way Bush was handling his job, and they voted for his Democratic opponent, John Kerry. After winning that difficult election, George W. Bush promised Americans that he would unite and heal the country.

CHAPTER 1

BIG GEORGE, LITTLE GEORGE

WHEN GEORGE W. BUSH was running for president of the United States in 2000 and 2004, he liked to act like a "good ol' Texas boy." He liked to eat chili and wear cowboy hats and boots. He talked about how much he had in common with hardworking Americans.

George W. Bush *(above left)* was informal with his supporters on the campaign trail.

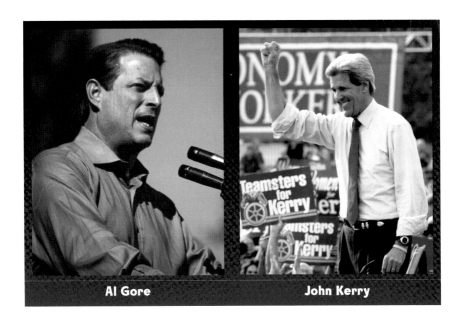

Al Gore   John Kerry

When people asked him questions, he gave simple answers. He made fun of his opponents (Al Gore in 2000 and John Kerry in 2004). Al Gore's father had been a U.S. senator. His family had a lot of money. John Kerry's father also had an important government job. And his relatives also had a lot of money. Al Gore and John Kerry both went to expensive high schools and universities. George W. made fun of these men's backgrounds. He said they did not understand real Americans. He said they only knew about powerful Americans who lived on the East Coast.

But George W. was a lot like Al Gore and John Kerry. His grandfather had been a U.S. senator. Other relatives were wealthy bankers and ran successful businesses. And even though George W. spoke with a Texas accent, he was not from Texas. In fact, he was born thousands of miles away, in New Haven, Connecticut.

George W.'s father is former U.S. president George Herbert Walker Bush. His mother is Barbara Bush. The two met in 1941 at a country club dance in Greenwich, Connecticut. Soon after that, George was sent to fight in World War II (1939–1945). He was a fighter pilot in the U.S. Navy. He fought bravely in the war. After being wounded in action, he married Barbara. His forehead carried a large bandage. It was covering a cut he had received while jumping from his burning airplane.

FAMOUS HERO

In 1944, Japanese gunfire hit George H. W. Bush's plane, which he had nicknamed Barbara. The plane went down. His crew, which was made up of a radioman and a weapons officer, was killed during the attack. Bush parachuted out of the plane into the icy cold Pacific Ocean. He was in danger of being eaten by sharks. But a submarine rescued him. He returned to the United States as a hero and received several medals.

Barbara and George Herbert Walker Bush on their wedding day

After they married, George and Barbara lived in New Haven, Connecticut. George went to Yale University. On July 6, 1946, their first son was born. They named him George Walker Bush. But as soon as he was born, people began calling him Little George. His father was known as Big George.

In 1948, Big George graduated from Yale. Then he faced a tough choice. He could follow his father and other relatives into the world of business and politics on the East Coast. Or he could set off and do something new on his own. Big George decided to set off on his own.

He moved his young family to western Texas. A lot of oil had been found in that part of the country. People were making money drilling for oil

George W. views the world from the shoulders of his proud father. Family members nicknamed them Big George and Little George.

and selling it. Good times in the oil industry are called an oil boom. Seeking to cash in on the boom, Big George took a job in the area. He worked as a clerk with one of the oil drilling companies. He rented a small apartment in the city of Odessa, Texas. It was all Big George could afford on a monthly salary of $375.

OIL TOWN

One year later, Big George's company moved the family to California. George W.'s sister, Pauline Robinson, was born there in 1949. Everybody called her Robin. The family returned to Texas the next year. They settled in Midland.

Midland was a dusty little town full of tumbleweeds. It was miles away from the nearest big city, and it often seemed like it was in the middle of nowhere. But Midland was the center of the oil boom. And the boom was so big that Midland soon became the richest town in the country.

IT'S A FACT!

In the 1950s, there were more luxury Rolls Royce cars per person in Midland than anywhere else in the United States.

A few years after moving to Midland, Big George started his own oil company. He called it the Zapata Petroleum Corporation. The name came from Emiliano Zapata, a famous fighter in the 1921 Mexican Revolution. Big George chose the name after seeing a popular movie called *Viva Zapata,* starring Marlon Brando.

Zapata Petroleum became a successful oil company. Big George earned a lot of money. The Bush family bought their first house. It was a two-bedroom home on a street nicknamed "Easter Egg Row." It got that name from the colorful houses up and down the street. The houses were built so much alike that the owners painted them bright colors to tell them apart. The Bush home was painted bright blue. Soon Zapata Petroleum became even more successful. In a few years, the family moved to a better neighborhood and a better house. This house had a swimming pool.

George W. was a very active child. Friends and relatives remember that he was always up to something. He went to Sam Houston Elementary School. He was the class clown. He made lots of jokes. People liked him, and he liked being the center of attention. After school, he played catcher

IT'S A FACT!

George W. loved baseball. One season he was good enough to be chosen as one of Midland's Little League All-Star players.

on his Little League baseball team. He spent his free time swimming in the family's pool and riding bikes. On weekends, he enjoyed family barbecues. Everything in Midland seemed to be going well.

FAMILY TRAGEDY

In 1952, when Little George was in first grade, his sister Robin became sick. Doctors discovered she had cancer. But Big George and Barbara decided not to tell Little George how very ill his sister was. It was a tough choice. Years later, Barbara Bush said, "We thought he was too young to cope."

When Little George was in second grade, his parents took Robin to see a special doctor in New York. They were gone for several months. Other relatives looked after Little George, but he missed his parents and his sister. He looked forward to them coming home. But Robin died in October 1953, while they were in New York.

George didn't find out until his parents came home. They went to pick him up from school. Out of the school window, Little George saw his parents' car. He ran to a teacher to tell her that he had to go because his parents and sister were waiting for him. "I run over to the car and there's no Robin," Bush recalled years later. Then his parents told him that Robin had died.

Later, as an adult, George W. Bush remembered how sad he had been when Robin died. He said her death was the only low point in his otherwise happy childhood. "I was sad, and stunned," Bush later said. "I knew Robin had been sick, but death was hard for me to imagine."

Little George W. poses with his younger sister Robin and their father. Robin had leukemia, a type of cancer. This type hits blood cells and can develop very quickly.

He remembered, "Minutes before, I had had a little sister, and now, suddenly, I did not." Little George was upset by Robin's death. But he was also angry because his parents had not told him how sick Robin was. For a long time, he had nightmares about his sister's death.

Little George's parents also struggled with their own grief. Barbara Bush had a hard time coming to terms with this sad situation. Everybody noticed how sad Little George's mother had become. Soon nobody said Robin's name inside the Bush home. They did not want to make Barbara Bush sadder.

It was Little George who finally made his mother smile again. He had just learned about how Earth spins on its axis. So one day after school, he asked his mother which way Robin had been buried in her grave. "What difference would it make?" his mother asked him. "One way she'd be spinning like this," he said, showing what he meant by turning himself around in one direction. "And one way like this," he said, turning in the opposite direction. Barbara Bush laughed at her son.

2

SCHOOL DAZE

IN 1959, when Little George was fourteen, his life changed in a big way. His family—which had come to include four more children—moved from Midland to the big city of Houston, Texas. In Midland, Little George had been class president and quarterback of the school football team. In Houston, he didn't know anyone at first. But he quickly made friends. He went to a private school called Kincaid School. He became a class officer and also joined the school football team.

IT'S A FACT!

By 1959, Bush had become the older brother to John (known as Jeb), Neil, Marvin, and Dorothy (Doro).

In 1961, Little George's life changed again. His parents sent him away to boarding school in Andover, Massachusetts. George Herbert Walker Bush had graduated from Phillips Academy in Andover. He and Barbara wanted their son to follow in his footsteps. They took him on a visit to Andover and enrolled him in the private school. The move was a turning point in Little George's life. For the first time, he had to make his way without his family around to support him.

Little George and his friends didn't understand why he had to move away from Texas. As an adult, Bush remembered that one friend had asked him, "Bush, what did you do wrong?" In those days in Texas, boys who got sent away to school were usually in trouble with their parents. But, as Bush later explained: "In my case, Andover was a family tradition. My parents wanted me to learn not only the

IT'S A FACT!

Life at Phillips Academy was a challenge for George. Before this, he'd been able to do pretty much as he pleased. This informal life was replaced by strict rules and regulations. Bush remembers "it was a shock to my system."

academics but also how to thrive on my own."
Little George wanted to make his parents happy.
But he did not enjoy his new school. He missed his
friends and family.

And Little George had another problem:
living up to his father's example. His father had
been a star athlete, a near-perfect student, and
president of the senior class. When he graduated,
the older Bush did not go straight to college.
Instead, he joined the military. He became the
youngest pilot in the U.S. Navy in World War II.
When he returned home, he attended Yale
University. After he graduated, he started his own
company. At school, teachers were always
comparing Little George to his father. Not only
did they have the same name, they also looked a
lot alike. And sometimes Little George acted just
like his father too. Some people even called him
Junior, even though his name was not George
Bush Jr. Sometimes George W. got tired of hearing
about how much everybody loved his father.

POPULAR GUY

Little George did find something to love at Phillips,
though. He loved playing stickball. Stickball is a

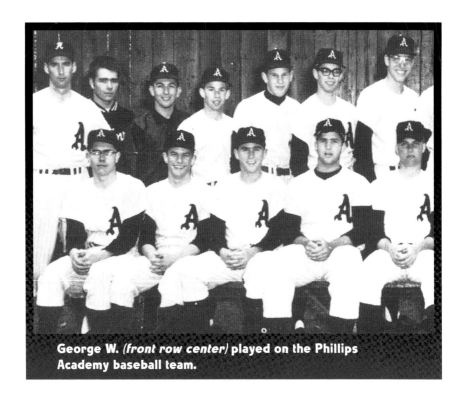

George W. *(front row center)* played on the Phillips Academy baseball team.

game that is similar to baseball. In the 1950s and 1960s, kids often played stickball in the streets of New York. Players use a broom handle or other long wooden stick to bat a small rubber ball to score runs. Little George created a stickball league at school. He got everyone on campus to join. He was in charge of the league. He set up a schedule of games and playoffs. He also played varsity basketball and baseball. He was not considered a star on the field, but he worked hard.

Little George did not do so well in the classroom. In fact, he did so badly that he was afraid he was going to flunk out of school. The first essay he wrote in an English class was a complete failure. He misused big words that he did not understand. The teacher gave him a zero on his report. "And my math grades weren't all

This is George W.'s 1964 yearbook photo. He was in his senior year at Phillips Academy.

that good either," Bush said years later. "So I was struggling."

Although he never made the honor roll, Little George was popular on campus. He made friends easily. He became the head cheerleader for the football team at the all-boys school. When he graduated from Phillips, he was popular enough to finish second in the election for Big Man on Campus.

After graduating from Phillips Academy, George had to decide which college to attend. He did not enjoy being away from home. And he didn't really like living on the East Coast. But he wanted to follow in his father's footsteps and go to Yale University. However, his grades did not seem high enough to get accepted into such a good school. He applied to Yale anyway. But he also applied to the University of Texas. The University of Texas was

IT'S A FACT!

At Phillips Academy, George W. was a member of a rock-and-roll band called the Torqueys. But he didn't play an instrument. His job was to stand on stage and clap his hands.

also a good school, but it was not as hard to get into as Yale was.

George did not have excellent grades, but he had something that helped him get into Yale anyway. Both his father and his grandfather had gone to Yale. Because he was the relative of Yale graduates, the school accepted him as a student. He set off for Yale in the fall of 1964 to study history. He soon found himself in the middle of history.

IT'S A FACT!

In the 1960s, students who got into Yale needed good scores on a national test called the Scholastic Aptitude Test (SAT). Those who got in had an average SAT score of 718 in math and 668 in the verbal part. Bush's scores were a bit lower with 640 in math and a verbal score of 566.

3 AT YALE

George W.
(above) at
Yale
University.
He was
often
annoyed by
the school's
rich-kid
atmosphere.

GEORGE W. ARRIVED at Yale in 1964.
By this time, the United States had become
involved in the Vietnam War (1957–1975).
Some Americans were beginning to question
the U.S. government's decision to send
troops to this war. Many people did not
agree with the war. Changing attitudes
seemed to be everywhere.

24

Around the country, life was changing in other ways. Until the 1960s, most men in the United States kept their hair cut short. But in the mid-1960s, young men began letting their hair grow. To many, longer hair was a symbol of rebellion against the war. To others, it was a way of saying they were not like their fathers or other older Americans. During the four years that Bush was at Yale (1964 to 1968), more and more college students were growing their hair long. Bush once said, "We later joked that members of the class of 1968 were the last in a long time to have short hair."

STARTING AT YALE

At Yale, George W. was very much aware of the changes around the country. When he arrived, in 1964, his father was running for the U.S. Congress. George H. W. Bush was a member of the Republican Party. He did not support the Civil Rights Act, a law that banned discrimination based on a person's race, religion, or nation of origin. He did support the Vietnam War. Many teachers and students at Yale did not support the war, but they did believe in the civil rights laws. Because of

CIVIL RIGHTS

For hundreds of years, African Americans did not have the same rights as other white Americans. For example, they couldn't eat in the same restaurants or sit in the same parts of a train. These are examples of discrimination, or hurtful and unfair practices toward another group.

In 1964, President Lyndon Johnson signed the Civil Rights Act. This law prevented discrimination based on a person's race, religion, or country of origin. By preventing discrimination, it guaranteed some new rights to African Americans, such as the right to use public facilities like restrooms and trains. But many Americans did not agree with the law. Others did not think it did enough to protect the rights of African Americans. These two groups of people often clashed with each other in the mid-1960s.

this, they did not respect George W.'s father. And many of them were not afraid to tell young George how they felt about his father.

Perhaps because of events like this, George W. decided he did not like many of the people at Yale. He felt they often pretended they were better than everybody else. He also thought they were too proud of going to a school like Yale. George W. did not like to act like he was better than anybody. He often wore wrinkled clothes and drove an old, beat-up car.

In his freshman (first) year at Yale, George W. pitched for the Yale baseball team.

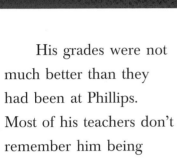

His grades were not much better than they had been at Phillips. Most of his teachers don't remember him being involved in a lot of academic activities. Instead, he spent a lot of time playing sports and having fun. As a freshman, he was a pitcher on the Yale baseball team. Two years later, he began to play rugby, a game that is a lot like football.

TROUBLE AT COLLEGE

But George W. found himself with a problem at Yale. He began drinking too much alcohol. He joined the Delta Kappa Epsilon (DKE) fraternity, which is a social club for male students. Fraternity members are called brothers. Most DKE brothers were athletes. They were known for drinking a lot of beer. Most of them lived together in the DKE house. The house was famous for having the loudest parties on the Yale campus. George H.W. Bush had been president of DKE in the 1940s. In the 1960s, George W. followed in his father's footsteps as DKE president.

FRATERNITIES

Most colleges and universities have separate social groups for men and women. The men's organization is called a fraternity (from the Latin word for "brother"). The women's group is called a sorority (from the Latin word for "sister"). The same fraternity can have a chapter, or branch, at different universities. A first-year student, or freshman, cannot apply to be part of a fraternity. Leaders of the group must invite a student to join. Freshmen who are invited to join a fraternity are called pledges.

Each fraternity or sorority gets its name from letters of the Greek alphabet. George Bush's fraternity was Delta Kappa Epsilon (or DKE). These are the fourth, tenth, and fifth letters of the Greek alphabet.

Students at Yale created the first DKE chapter in 1844. Its members were to be "in equal [parts] the gentleman, the scholar, and the jolly good-fellow." DKE has more than forty-five active chapters in the United States. Five U.S. presidents were members of DKE. These members were Gerald Ford, Theodore Roosevelt, Rutherford B. Hayes, and both George Bushes.

In his last year, Bush became the DKE president. In this role, he continued to go by the rules of "the jolly good-fellow." He and the fraternity became known for their wild actions. One fraternity brother remembered that DKE was a lot like the movie *Animal House*. He said George was close to John "Bluto" Blutarksy, the character played by John Belushi. In the movie, Bluto is the wildest and most fun-loving person of the group.

The fraternity brothers at DKE did some crazy stunts. A few times, they got into trouble with their teachers and even the police. One night, George W. had too much to drink at a party. While walking home, he suddenly lay down in the middle of the street. Then he began rolling himself home. Another time, he went with some friends to a football game at Princeton, another university on the East Coast. Yale won the game.

It's a Fact!

One of George's DKE brothers was Calvin Hill. Hill later became a professional football player with the Dallas Cowboys. Hill said, "George was a fraternity guy." He meant that George W. behaved wildly, just like most other college students who belonged to fraternities.

To celebrate, George W. and his friends tore down the goalpost after the game. "We charged onto the field to take the goal post down," Bush remembered. "Unfortunately, I was sitting on the crossbar when campus security arrived. The police were not nearly as impressed with our victory as we were. We were escorted off the field and told to leave town. I have not been back since."

That wasn't the only time George W. got into trouble with the police during his college years. One year, during the Christmas holiday, he and some friends stole a Christmas wreath from a department store. The police caught them and arrested them. George W. said he had just been "borrowing" the wreath. The police arrested him anyway. But later they dropped the charges. George W. and his friends had to apologize to the store owners.

Many of George's friends from those days agree that he had a wild side. But, they say, he never did anything too terrible. For instance, he never did anything so bad that he couldn't one day become president of the United States. In fact, most of his trouble could be blamed on two things–drinking too much alcohol and being too young to make good decisions.

MORE TROUBLE

At Yale, George W. had a lot of friends, both men and women. But he only went on a few dates. However, one time he got into trouble with his dad because of a girlfriend. One summer while in college, George W. got a job on an oil ship in the Gulf of Mexico. He was dating a girl in Houston at the time, and he missed being with her. Since he would be heading back to college soon, he wanted to spend more time with her. So he quit his job and returned to Houston to be with her. His father did not like this. He called George W. into his Houston office. He told him how disappointed he was with the choice the young man had made. George W. broke up with that girl a short time later.

But soon he found a new romance. During the Christmas break of his junior (third) year at Yale, he got engaged to Cathryn Wolfman. She was a student at Rice University in Houston. George W. was twenty, the same age his father had been when he'd become engaged. George W. and Wolfman had fun together in Houston. But soon George W. had to return to Yale. The couple drifted apart. They broke up soon after that.

In 1967, George W. was mentioned in an article in the *New York Times*. The story was about an activity called "branding" that DKE fraternity brothers did to pledges (pledges are people who are seeking to join a fraternity). Often, fraternity brothers force pledges to do crazy stunts—an enforcement that many would call bullying—to prove they are worthy of joining the group. The DKE fraternity brothers used a piece of heated metal to burn, or "brand," the skin of pledges. Somehow, newspaper reporters found out about the activity. They wrote about it in newspapers. Many people were angry that the DKE members would harm their fellow students by burning them. Reporters from the *New York Times* interviewed George W. about branding. He said it did not really hurt the pledges. He said it was no worse than cigarette burns.

SECRET SOCIETY

Like his father before him, George W. joined the secret Skull and Bones Society at Yale. Skull and Bones is a secret club that chooses the top fifteen Yale students to join each year. The members are called Bonesmen. Skull and Bones is called a secret society because Bonesmen are not allowed to talk about what they do as members of the club. George W.'s father had been a Bonesman. The older Bush had been chosen because he was a war hero.

George W. was not one of the top fifteen Yale students. He was not a war hero like his father. But he was invited to join Skull and Bones anyway. He was allowed to join as a legacy. A legacy is someone who is asked to join because that person's father was a Bonesman.

SKULL AND BONES

Mystery surrounds Yale University's Skull and Bones Society. Created in the 1830s, the society invites the best and brightest of the junior class to join. Each year, fifteen students become members. Part of their initiation is a vow of secrecy and lifetime loyalty to the society.

Most members, called Bonesmen, come from well-respected, wealthy families. Some have moved on to become gifted leaders. Originally an all-male organization, the society started inviting women to become members in 1991. Two times a week, students in the society meet in a stone building often called "the tomb." Little is known of what the members talk about or do in the tomb.

Bonesmen don't talk about the society. Even saying the words "skull and bones" around a nonmember is looked down upon. Very few people even claim to be members. Known members include President George W. Bush, his father, and both of his grandfathers. Another member is John Kerry, who ran against Bush in the 2004 presidential election.

Some Bonesmen have not kept their vow of secrecy. They have described parts of the society to the media. These former members have said the society has used its influence to put its members into jobs with a lot of power. But not much evidence can be found to support these claims.

Yale's Skull and Bones tomb

IT'S A FACT!

Bonesmen have secret names. Bush's name was "Temporary" because he couldn't come up with a permanent secret name for himself.

Bonesmen have to promise to keep Skull and Bones activities a secret. But some members have talked to newspaper reporters over the years. The reporters promised not to mention the members' names.

Throughout the late 1960s, male college students spent a lot of time thinking about what they would do if they were drafted into the Vietnam War. During the 1960s, the United States required all capable young men to join the armed forces (the U.S. Army, Navy, Air Force, or Marines). In a draft, the government selects young men (no women were drafted) to fight.

THINKING ABOUT VIETNAM

During the Vietnam War, many young men who were not in college or who had finished college were drafted. Young men in college got a deferment that put off their being drafted. But many of these young people did not support the war. They did not want to be drafted now or ever.

U.S. Marines wade across a river in Vietnam.

Some young men even moved to Canada to avoid being drafted.

George W.'s friends remember that he always had supported the war. George W.'s father, who was now Congressman George H. W. Bush, was in favor of the war. Some of George W.'s friends didn't like that Congressman Bush wanted war. And they remember that George W. always stood by his father's position.

Martin Luther King Jr.   **Senator Robert Kennedy**

George W. graduated from Yale in 1968. That same year, Dr. Martin Luther King Jr.–a famous civil rights leader–was shot and killed. A few months later, Senator Robert Kennedy–who also fought for civil rights and was against the war in Vietnam–was also killed. Many college students and other Americans were angry about these killings.

At the same time, the Vietnam War was dragging on. Thousands of U.S. soldiers were dying. Young Bush later said that the year 1968 changed his world. Until then, he had been carefree. But that year, he had to begin thinking about the Vietnam War and other serious issues. George W. realized that as soon as he graduated, he could be drafted and sent to Vietnam. Some of his friends decided to leave the United States and move to Canada rather than be drafted.

But George W. didn't want to do that. He was the son of a congressman, and he was proud of his country. Still, like many other young men, he didn't want to go to Vietnam to fight. Instead, he joined the Texas Air National Guard to train to be a soldier. But he would probably not go to Vietnam because members of the Guard were not often sent to war zones.

4

THE WILD BLUE YONDER

BUSH WAS TWENTY-TWO YEARS OLD
when he joined the Texas Air National Guard.
The Air National Guard is a reserve unit of
the U.S. military. This means the unit is
called to fight wars only after the regular U.S.
Army and U.S. Air Force have been used. Air
National Guard members learn to fly fighter
planes in case they are called to go to war.

Bush said he wanted to be a fighter pilot
like his father had been in World War II. His
father had often told him how much he
enjoyed flying planes. The younger Bush had
never flown a plane before he joined the Air
National Guard. After he graduated from
college, he knew he would probably be
drafted if he didn't make a decision about the
National Guard. He later said, "I wanted to

Some saw George W.'s service in the Texas Air National Guard as a way to escape combat in Vietnam. George W. says that he just wanted to be a military pilot.

learn a new skill that would make doing my duty an interesting adventure. I had never flown an airplane but decided I wanted to become a pilot."

GETTING INTO THE NATIONAL GUARD

Some people said that Bush only joined the Air National Guard so he wouldn't have to go to Vietnam. As a reserve unit, the National Guard members would be less likely to be sent to Vietnam than regular soldiers were. And National Guard pilots flew older planes than the regular U.S.

Air Force did. So even if a Guard unit did get sent to Vietnam, they probably wouldn't have to fly in battle. The air force had better fighter jets to fight with.

IT'S A FACT!

In the Air National Guard, Bush piloted the T-37, the T-38, and the F-102A. The T-37 and T-38 are trainers, although the T-38 is the faster of the two airplanes. The F-102A is a fast interceptor aircraft. This means that its job is to find and destroy enemy planes.

Some people also said that Bush should not have been accepted into the Guard. They said that a lot of other young men also wanted to join the National Guard. To join the Guard, a person has to pass a difficult test. Bush got the lowest score you could get and still be accepted. People said that other young men scored higher than Bush and did not get in. They said Bush got in only because his father was a congressman. Also, Bush had not filled out his application correctly. He left one part blank. It was the part asking him to list any trouble he had been in with police.

But Bush said he did not use any special favors to get into the Guard. He said he must have forgotten to fill out the missing part of the application. And, he said, he scored high enough on the test to get in. In fact, he said, a lot of people his age did not want to join the Guard. When you joined the Guard, you had to remain a part of the Guard for almost six years. Many young men preferred to go to Vietnam for one year and then to be finished with their military service. Bush said he chose to join the Guard because it was the fastest way to become a fighter pilot, like his father had been.

After Bush entered the Air National Guard, he became the center of a lot of attention. The attention began during his very first weeks as a National Guardsman. When a person is accepted into the Guard, there is a "swearing-in" ceremony. This is when the person promises to do his service and obey orders. Bush was sworn in on the same day he applied. But his commander held a special ceremony weeks later. The commander wanted newspaper photographers to take his picture with the congressman's son.

Later, Bush was promoted to lieutenant. His commander held another ceremony for the newspapers. This time, the commander invited

Congressman Bush. The congressman flew from Washington, D.C., to Houston to have his picture taken with his son and the commander. Soon after that, Bush went to Georgia to begin his two years of Air National Guard training.

MORE ATTENTION

In Georgia, Bush began to get even more attention, from even more important people. In 1968, Richard Nixon had been elected president. George

The elder Bush *(right)* proudly presents his son with the bars signifying his promotion to second lieutenant in the Air National Guard.

W.'s father, Congressman Bush, had worked hard to
help Nixon win votes in Texas. Once he was
president, Nixon rewarded the congressman by
giving him some important government positions.
Many people knew that President Nixon and
Congressman Bush were becoming friends.

Some people began to think that the
congressman's son was getting special favors. For
instance, most National Guardsmen could not take
any vacation while they were training. But Bush
was allowed to take two months off. He went to
Florida to work for a friend's election. And the next
year, President Nixon sent a special air force plane
to Bush's training camp in Georgia. The plane
picked up Bush and flew him to Washington. Bush
had been invited to take out the president's
daughter Tricia. Bush's friends in the Air National
Guard liked to kid him about his date with the
president's daughter. They started calling him a
"ladies' man."

5

THE SCHOOL OF HARD KNOCKS

LIFE IN THE GUARD WAS FULL of hard work and hard playing. During the week, National Guardsmen worked, studied, and trained to fly fighter jets. On the weekends, they went out in the local town. In those days, Bush often drank too much alcohol. But in June 1970, he graduated from Air National Guard Training School. He would serve for four years as a part-time National Guardsman.

After finishing training school, Bush moved back to Texas. At the age of twenty-four, he was handsome and fun to be around. He was also a little bit famous because of his father. Many people wanted to be friends with him, and a lot of young women wanted to date him. Bush rented a one-bedroom apartment in an apartment complex in Houston. The complex was popular with young, single people. It had six swimming pools and lots of parties. Since he only had to report for Guard duty on the weekends, Bush had a lot of free time. He had not decided what he wanted to do with his life. He spent many days playing all-day pool volleyball with his friends.

FINDING DIRECTION

In 1971, Bush's family—his parents and younger brothers and sister—moved to New York. President Nixon had offered George H. W. Bush an important job with the United Nations, an organization that

The elder Bush, *right*, appears with Paul Eggers, *left*, the candidate for governor of Texas, and with Republican president Richard Nixon, *center*, at a campaign rally.

works for world peace. The younger Bush stayed in Houston. He still didn't know what he wanted to do for a job. A family friend gave him a job selling farm equipment. It was the first real job that Bush had ever held. He had to go to work at 9 A.M. five days a week. He had to wear a coat and a tie every day. He hated the job. He stayed only about nine months.

He began thinking about going into politics, like his father and grandfather. He thought about running for the Texas legislature, the group that makes laws for that state. The Bush family name was well known in Houston. People were interested to learn that the younger Bush might run for political office. The *Houston Post* newspaper wrote a story about George W. Bush, but they called him George Bush Jr.

Bush still found it hard to always be compared to his father. Once while visiting his parents' house, he had a big fight with his dad. The fight began after the younger Bush took his sixteen-year-old brother, Marvin, out for a drive. Bush had been drinking beer, and he was drunk. When he was driving home with Marvin, he ran over a neighbor's garbage cans. One can stuck under the car, but Bush kept driving. It made a loud clunking and scratching noise. When he pulled up to his parents' house, the noise woke his father up. His father was upset because Bush had been driving drunk. And he was also upset that his son had damaged the car and made such a loud noise.

Father and son got into a heavy argument. Bush even tried to get his father to fight him. His father was able to calm him down. But Big George was worried about his son. He thought he drank too much alcohol. He thought he needed to settle down with a job or at least have a plan for his future.

The younger Bush also knew it was time to settle down. He decided to return to school to get his graduate degree. He applied to Harvard Business School in Cambridge, Massachusetts. Harvard Business School is one of the best schools in the country, and only a small number of people who apply get

IT'S A FACT!

Before Bush decided to apply to Harvard Business School, he thought about becoming a lawyer. He applied to the University of Texas Law School but was turned down.

accepted. He wouldn't find out if he was accepted for several months.

A LOOK AT A DIFFERENT SIDE

Bush's father was worried that his son might get into trouble while he waited. And he also wanted his son to see another side of life. He wanted him to know that not everybody was as fortunate as he was. So the older Bush talked to his friend, John L. White.

White was a former professional football player. He had started a group called Professional United Leadership League (PULL). PULL helped poor kids who lived in Houston's toughest neighborhoods. The program provided adults for the kids to talk to. PULL owned an old warehouse that it used as a recreation center for the kids. The kids played sports and learned arts and crafts. Bush was hired as a counselor. That meant he talked to the kids about life and tried to help them solve problems.

Bush was great at his new job. The kids and the other workers loved him. He wrestled with the kids, played basketball with them, and took them on field trips. He found it easy to relate to the children. In many ways, he was still a big, fun-loving kid himself. A man Bush worked with remembered him as a great guy: "If he was a stinker, I'd say he was a stinker. But everybody loved him so much. He had a way with people." Other coworkers remember him that way too. They also remember that he drove around in a beat-up old car. The car was full of clothes and papers. It was so full that no one else could fit inside it.

Bush also learned a lot at PULL. It made him sad to see how hard the kids' lives were. Once he played basketball with an eleven-year-old. When the child jumped to shoot the ball, a loaded pistol fell out of his pocket. The child thought he needed the gun for protection. Bush was saddened to know that children lived like this. But he also found some happiness. He became friends with a boy named Jimmy. Jimmy became like a little brother to Bush. Each day, the boy waited for Bush to arrive and then followed him everywhere.

One day, Jimmy showed up at the center without shoes, so Bush bought him a pair. When he walked the boy home, Jimmy's mother was high on drugs. "Jimmy was happy to be home, but I was incredibly sad to leave him there," Bush said. He added that his job let him see a part of the world that he had never seen before. It made him both happy and sad at the same time. "I saw a lot of poverty. I also saw bad choices: drugs, alcohol, abuse. . . . I saw children who could not read or write and were way behind in school." But he also saw good people who worked hard to give their children a good life. This made him happy and hopeful for the children.

IT'S A FACT!

Marvin Bush joined his older brother working at PULL in inner-city Houston. The two brothers were the only white people working in the building. "They stood out like sore thumbs," said Muriel Simmons Henderson, another PULL counselor.

While working at PULL, Bush found out that he had been accepted to Harvard. He liked his work with the kids so much that he didn't want to quit. He thought about staying at PULL and not going to Harvard. But John White convinced him to go to school. "If you really care about these kids as much as I think you do, why don't you go and learn more and then you can really help," White told Bush.

GOING TO HARVARD

Bush arrived at Harvard looking for some direction in his life. He was twenty-seven years old. Many Harvard students become powerful businesspeople. Others become government leaders. In those days, these serious students often wore suits to class. But Bush didn't look like a powerful leader. He arrived at the school driving his dumpy car. It was still full of clothes and papers. He wore casual clothes that were often wrinkled. In one famous yearbook photo, Bush is shown sitting at the back of a classroom. He is wearing a badly wrinkled shirt, chewing gum, and blowing a large bubble.

Bush may have had a casual attitude, but he took his studies seriously. He learned about finance, marketing, and other things needed to run a business. Two years later, he graduated with his master's degree in business administration. Then he surprised many people when he followed the path his father had taken twenty-five years earlier. George W. Bush loaded up his car and drove west to Texas. He wanted to make his fortune in the oil fields.

CHAPTER 6
IN THE OIL BUSINESS

BUSH HAD GROWN UP around the oil business. But he had no experience running an oil company. With his degree from Harvard, he could have gotten a job as a manager at an oil company. But he decided he wanted to learn about the business from the bottom up. So in 1975, he took a job as a land man.

A land man looks up records in county courthouses to see who owns what properties. Bush traveled all over west Texas looking up records. His job was to try to get the owners to lease or sell the land to a company drilling for oil. Bush had a good personality for this kind of job. He loved to talk to people. He could drive up to homes and start conversations with complete strangers. And he learned a lot from this job. Soon he felt like he knew enough to

Workers tend to a Texas oil rig. Midland's oil production boomed in the 1970s.

start his own oil business. He chose to start it in Midland, the town where he had grown up. [N18]

At about the same time, Bush decided to run for Congress. He had worked on some of his father's elections. So he had a good idea of how to run a campaign. A popular congressman from the area had decided to leave his seat in Congress. Bush decided he had a good chance of winning the election.

He entered the race as a Republican, the same political party as his father. Bush's father was very happy to have his eldest son enter politics. It was a Bush family tradition, after all. Lots of family and friends came to Midland to help on the campaign. Bush's younger brother Neil had just finished college. He came to help his brother run for Congress. An old friend named Joe O'Neill also helped in the campaign.

MEETING LAURA

George W. announced he would run for Congress in August 1977. That same month, Joe O'Neill and his wife, Jan, invited him to a barbecue. There, Bush met Laura Welch, a quiet elementary school librarian. Laura loved books and learning, but she had no interest in politics. At first, it didn't seem like Bush and Laura had much in common. He loved to be surrounded by people. He was always laughing and liked to be the life of any party. She was quiet and liked to read.

IT'S A FACT!

When his family was still living in Midland, George lived only a half mile away from Laura Welch. They even went to the same junior high school.

But they liked each other from the minute they met. The next night, they went to play miniature golf. In October, Bush took Laura to Houston to meet his family. Less than three months later, on November 5, 1977, George W. and Laura Bush

George W. and Laura Bush on their wedding day, November 5, 1977. *Left to right:* **Marvin, Dorothy, Neil, Columb (Jeb's wife), Jeb, Laura, George W., Barbara, George, and Dorothy Walker Bush (George W.'s grandmother).**

were married. The wedding was in Midland at the First United Methodist Church.

Shortly after the wedding, Bush went back to work on his campaign for U.S. Congress. He promised Laura that she would not have to make any speeches. Laura did not like speaking in front of crowds. But she knew that the wife of a politician would have to make speeches. A few months later, she made her first campaign speech

Newlyweds George W. and Laura campaigned side by side when George W. ran for Congress.

in Muleshoe, Texas. Laura was terrified, but she turned out to be a good speaker.

In June 1978, Bush won the Republican primary election against all the other Republicans trying to win. This election decides which Republican candidate will run in the general election in the fall. Both major political parties—the Democrats and the Republicans—hold primary elections to choose their candidates for the general election.

The general election was set for November 1978. Bush ran against Democrat Kent Hance. Bush had already learned a lot about campaigning from his father. But he learned even more in his own first real campaign. Hance told voters that Bush was not really a Texan. He reminded voters that Bush had been born in Connecticut. He talked about how he had gone to schools on the East Coast. Hance said

that his own father and grandfather had been
farmers in Texas for decades. Hance easily won the
election.

Bush was disappointed to lose the election, but
he didn't dwell on it. He decided to get back into
the oil business. He started his own oil drilling
company. He called it Arbusto–the Spanish word for
"bush" or "shrub." Bush family friends helped him
start the business. They raised millions of dollars to
buy equipment, to rent offices, and to hire workers.
Bush's workers said he was a good boss. He treated
people fairly. He let people do their jobs. He didn't
always think that he knew more than anybody else.
His company was successful. In the late 1970s and
early 1980s, oil prices were high. This meant oil
companies could make large profits.

FAMILY SUCCESS

In 1980, Bush stopped working to help his father
with his political goals. Big George was running in
the Republican primary for president. He wanted to
defeat President Jimmy Carter, leader of the
Democratic Party. Carter was a peanut farmer from
Georgia. He had been governor of Georgia before he
was president. The United States went through some

difficult times while Carter was president. Gas prices were high. The cost of other goods was rising quickly. Millions of people couldn't find jobs. Adding to the problem, sixty-six U.S. citizens had been taken hostage by Iranian terrorists in Iran on November 4, 1979. During the 1980 election season, the terrorists were still holding fifty-two of them at the U.S. Embassy in Teheran, Iran. Carter's government had tried and failed to free them several times. Because of this, many people did not want Carter to be president again.

IT'S A FACT!

Thirteen of the Iranian hostages had been released in late 1979. One more was released in 1980. The remaining fifty-two were held for over fourteen months.

Bush's father did not win the chance to run for president for the Republican Party. But the winner, Ronald Reagan, did select the older Bush as his vice-presidential running mate. In the November general election, the Reagan-Bush ticket won the presidency. The younger Bush, with his wife Laura, went to Washington, D.C., to see his father take the oath of office as vice president of the United States. The younger Bush was filled with pride.

He felt that same emotion the following November, when Laura gave birth to twin daughters. The happy parents named the girls Jenna Welch, for Laura's mother, and Barbara Pierce, for Bush's mother. Bush helped with the feeding and the changing of diapers, and he took the babies for walks in the stroller.

In the meantime, he began thinking about getting back into a political race. He considered running for governor of Texas. This surprised even his family. They wondered if he had the necessary experience for such a high office. Barbara Bush told her son that he was probably not ready to run for governor. Bush was angry to hear this from his mother, but he listened.

George W. holds his twin daughters, Barbara Pierce, *left*, and Jenna Welch, *right*, born in November 1981.

BUSINESS FAILURE

Instead of going into politics, Bush worked hard keeping his oil company in business. He was not as successful as his father had been. By 1982, the oil industry began to go into a slump. Oil companies were no longer making the huge profits they had been making in the 1970s.

In 1984, Bush merged Arbusto with a larger oil exploration company called Spectrum 7. By 1985, the price of oil had dropped from $25 per barrel to $9 per barrel. Companies and fortunes were wiped out. Bush's company was among those suffering in west Texas. The company was on the verge of bankruptcy. In 1985, it owed $1.6 million to the bank. Luckily, Bush was once again rescued by his name and family connections. As Bush himself said, "I'm all name and no money."

The rescuer was a big company named Harken Oil and Gas. The company wanted to use the Bush name and family connections. So Harken bought Spectrum 7 in 1986 and paid off the company's large debts. Harken also hired many of the former Spectrum employees. Bush was hired for $120,000 a year. But at the same time, Bush's father was running for president. Bush was working full-time on his father's campaign, so he wasn't actually working much for Harken. He was made a member of Harken's board of directors and received $300,000 of Harken stock. These are paper certificates that give the person part ownership of the company. A company's stock can be worth a lot of money.

Bush earned hundreds of thousands of dollars from the Harken deal. Although he was finally set financially, Bush had actually failed. His oil company had gone out of business. Just as he had tried and failed to follow in his father's footsteps at Andover and Yale, he also failed to match his father's business success.

IT'S A FACT!

After the Harken company bought Bush's oil business, somebody asked why Harken had paid Bush so much. Harken's founder replied: "What was Harken getting for its money? The son of the vice president of the United States. His name was George Bush. That was worth the money they paid him."

CHAPTER 7

HIGHBALLS AND HARDBALLS

IN THE MID-1980s, Bush was enjoying a happy life with his young family. But he had one major problem he needed to deal with—his excessive alcohol drinking. The drinking had been bothering Bush and his family most of his adult life. Once he became angry with a reporter for the *Wall Street Journal*. Bush swore at the reporter in public. He also often arrived at work with a hangover from drinking too much the night before. In looking back at his life, Bush says he was not an alcoholic. But he admits that he had a bad habit of drinking too much and then getting into arguments. In 1986, at the age of forty, Bush decided that enough was enough. He vowed to give up drinking.

Laura had been trying to get her husband to quit drinking for years. But a conversation with the Reverend Billy Graham, a family friend, got Bush thinking about changing his life. At the celebration of his fortieth birthday, Bush decided to quit drinking for good. The Bushes and some friends gathered at the Broadmoor Hotel in Colorado in June 1986 to celebrate several birthdays. The next morning, Bush went out for his usual jog. He felt so terrible after the run that he decided his body was trying to tell him he was getting too old to drink. He decided to stop right then. He claims he hasn't had a drink since.

The love and support of George W.'s family (shown here at George and Barbara Bush's home in Kennebunkport, Maine) helped him give up alcohol. George W. and Laura, with the twins, are the third and fourth adults from the left.

HELPING DAD

After deciding to stop drinking alcohol, Bush was faced with another tough decision. He didn't have a daily job, and he was once again looking for something to do with his life. In 1986 he joined his father's presidential campaign. The elder Bush had been vice president since 1980. He had decided to run for president in 1988, and he needed to start his campaign ahead of time to raise money and gain supporters.

Bush served as his father's "enforcer" on the campaign trail. He made sure that all the campaign workers were loyal to his father. It was a high-pressure job, and he often got into yelling matches with workers and journalists. This added to his growing reputation of having a bad temper. But he was determined to do the job he was hired to do. For example, he worked hard to encourage journalists to be favorable when they wrote about his father, the presidential candidate.

In 1988, the Republicans and the Democrats held their national conventions to confirm their presidential candidates. George W. became especially angry with Texas politician Ann Richards, the keynote speaker at the Democratic

National Convention. Richards was known for being a smart and funny speaker. During her speech, she portrayed the elder Bush as a weak politician. She said he had only succeeded because he had had things handed to him his whole life. She also poked fun at his habit of mispronouncing words. During her speech on national television, Richards said it really wasn't his fault. "Poor George," she said, "he can't help it. He was born with a silver foot in his mouth." (This is a funny version of the expression, "having a silver spoon in one's mouth." It describes someone who was born with the advantages of silver, or money.) The remark drew a huge laugh from the audience. But it upset the Bush family, especially the eldest son.

Ann Richards was the keynote speaker at the 1988 Democratic National Convention.

His father won the 1988 presidential election
that fall, and the victory made George W. better
known around the country. Once again, he
thought about getting into politics. He considered
running for governor of Texas in 1990. But he
decided that the race would be too close to his
father's election. Bush and Laura and the twins
occasionally visited the White House, but George
W. worked hard to show people he was not just
the president's son. For example, after his father
became president, George W. stopped working for
him. He did not accept any jobs in his father's
government. Most of his life, Bush had been
fighting the perception that he had gotten where
he was because of his father. If he was to have
any political future, he needed to do something to
establish himself on his own. So he decided to
choose the world of professional baseball.

BASEBALL CALLS

Bush had always been a huge fan of major league
baseball. As a child, he had collected baseball
cards. He had memorized batting averages and
home run statistics. He often pretended to be Willie
Mays, his favorite player. Later, he recalled that the

other kids in Midland were always impressed with his father's catching abilities. They especially liked the fact that Mr. Bush could catch a fly ball with his glove behind his back.

So, in 1989, Bush jumped at the chance to become part owner of the Texas Rangers baseball team. For his share, Bush paid $600,000. The total price for the team was $75 million, split among several buyers. Bush did not put in a lot of money, but he had something valuable to add to the buyers' group. Once again, his name and family history were important to the deal. Bush was asked to be the team's public spokesman and managing partner.

IT'S A FACT!

As a child, George W. had had one of the best baseball card collections in Texas. He was particularly pleased when, as part owner of the Texas Rangers, he got his own picture on a card.

Bush got the money for his share of the team by taking out a bank loan. As proof to the bank that he could repay the loan, Bush pointed to his Harken stocks. In 1990, he sold some of these stocks to pay off the loan. But the stock sale got him into some trouble. He had sold the stock on June 22, 1990, when the company's stock price was $4 a share. Bush made $835,000 on the sale. But two weeks later, the stock price dropped to less then $2.50 a share. Bush was on Harken's board of directors. Many people thought he probably knew that the price of the stock was going to drop. And if he did know that, it was against the law for him to sell his stock—with his unfair advantage of inside information—and make a big profit. Somebody complained about Bush's actions, and the Securities and Exchange Commission (SEC) investigated. (The SEC is a U.S. agency that enforces the laws about the purchase and sale of stocks and bonds.)

Bush said he had not known about Harken's money troubles. He insisted that he would not have sold the stock if he had known about the problems. He pointed out that Harken's lawyers had studied the sale and said it was okay. He also said that he hadn't found out about the money problems until a month after he sold the stock. The SEC investigators decided there was not enough evidence to charge Bush with a crime.

Meanwhile, Bush turned his attention to the Texas Rangers. The Rangers had never had much

George W. took on a new project by becoming part owner of the Texas Rangers baseball team.

success as a baseball team. They played near Dallas, Texas, and their biggest star was the legendary pitcher Nolan Ryan. Bush bought the team because he loved baseball. But it was also a smart move for his future in politics.

Owning the Rangers made Bush a famous Texas businessman. The newspapers talked about him often. And having his name in the newspaper would help him greatly if he decided to run for governor in 1994. The job with the Rangers also helped the people of Texas to get to know Bush. He asked his mother, then the First Lady of the United States, to throw out the first pitch at a Rangers' game. He spoke to community groups about the team every week. During each home

First Lady Barbara Bush throws the first pitch at a Rangers game.

game, he was in the stands. He signed thousands of autographs for fans.

While he was with the Rangers, Bush suffered only two big setbacks. The first was a sports world disappointment: the Rangers never won the World Series. The second was political. George W.'s father was not reelected president. Bill Clinton defeated the elder Bush in 1992, with 43 percent of the votes to 38 percent for Bush.

Bush and his fellow team owners had big success in building a new baseball stadium. In 1994, the $190-million stadium opened. This greatly increased the value of the team. It also helped Bush prove that he could come through on a major project.

8 "W" STANDS FOR WINNER

IN 1994, BUSH DECIDED to run for governor of Texas. Ann Richards, who had earlier poked fun at Bush's father, had been governor of Texas since 1990. Some of Bush's friends believed that one of the reasons he decided to run against Ann Richards was to get back at her for the jokes. "Ann made a name for herself and her tongue in 1988 by ridiculing my father," Bush said. "She built on that attention to mount a successful campaign for governor in 1990. But if she wants a second four-year term, her biggest roadblock is going to be another George Bush."

George W. ran for governor of Texas in 1994. Here he speaks to a crowd in Irving, Texas.

FACING THE CRITICS

At the time, Bush was well known in Texas and around the country as an owner of the Texas Rangers. But he realized he would have to be careful in his race against Richards. She was a popular governor. Richards also had a great sense of humor. She often showed this on television with talk-show hosts such as Jay Leno and David Letterman. Bush friends were afraid that Richards's style of joking would make Bush angry during the campaign. They were afraid that he would embarrass himself.

Bush had another problem besides Ann Richards's jokes. This problem was something that had often helped him throughout his life. It was his family name and his famous father. Now, Bush was afraid that people would think he had never done anything on his own. He was afraid people would think he was nothing more than the son of the former president. "My biggest problem in Texas is the question, 'What's the boy ever done? He could be riding his Daddy's name,'" Bush said before the campaign.

He decided to address the issue directly. He called a press conference to announce that he was running for governor. And he asked his parents to stay home. He did not want the press to give all their attention to the former president and First Lady. At his first campaign stop, he stated his reason for running for governor. "I am not running for governor because I am George Bush's son," he said. "I am running because I am Jenna and Barbara's father." Although Bush didn't let his father get involved in his campaign, his mother campaigned for him.

Bush focused on three main issues during the 1994 campaign. First, he wanted counties and cities in Texas to have more power in making decisions

IT'S A FACT!

Bush's brother Jeb ran for and lost the election for governor of Florida in 1994, the same year Bush won election in Texas. In 1998, when George W. Bush was reelected governor in Texas, Jeb won the job in Florida.

about public schools. Second, he wanted tougher punishment for kids who committed crimes. Last, he wanted to change the state's welfare system (the agencies that help poor people). He thought the state was wasting money in this system.

Bush also made a big decision about how he would treat Ann Richards personally during the campaign. As much as he disliked the current governor, Bush decided that the best way to defeat her was to ensure that he himself never attack her personally. "We're never going to attack her because she would be a fabulous victim," Bush said. "We're going to treat her with respect and dignity. This is how we are going to win." Bush didn't even show anger when Richards said Bush had gotten everything in life because of his father. Bush only criticized Richards's policies. He let his campaign people criticize Richards's personality.

GOVERNOR BUSH

The plan proved successful. Bush surprised many people around the country and won the election. He got 53 percent of the vote, and Richards got only 46 percent. Suddenly George W. Bush was the governor of one of the biggest states in the country. He quickly became a major figure in national politics. All he had to do was avoid being foolish in office, and people would continue to take him seriously.

The entire Bush family gathered in Texas to see George W. sworn in as governor. They had reason to be proud. Bush was the first Republican to be elected governor of Texas since 1877. The new governor, Laura, and the twins moved to Austin, Texas, to live in the stately governor's mansion. Bush was a good, but not great, governor. He focused on his three campaign issues: local control of education, harsher penalties for criminals, and changes to welfare. He also approved laws protecting businesses from big lawsuits.

Bush made no major mistakes while in office. As a result, many Republicans began to consider Bush as a possible presidential candidate for 1996. Bush was interested in running for president in 1996 for one big reason. He would run against Bill Clinton, the man who had defeated his father in 1992.

In the end, Bush decided not to run for president in 1996. But Republicans around the country hoped he would run in the year 2000. In 1998, Bush was reelected governor of Texas. He had learned how to appeal to many different kinds

Laura and George W. greet the public in an inaugural parade after his second election as governor of Texas.

of voters. In his victory speech, he described himself as a "compassionate conservative"–a term meaning he cared about people without spending a lot of money on social programs to help them.

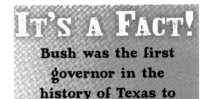

It's a Fact!

Bush was the first governor in the history of Texas to win two four-year terms in a row.

After winning reelection, Bush and his business partners decided to sell the Texas Rangers. They sold the team in 1998 for $250 million. As his part of the profits, Bush received almost $15 million. He was set financially for life. He could now focus on seeking the Republican nomination for president in 2000. His friend Joe O'Neill told him, "Congratulations. You hit the long ball. Now you can run for president. . . . You're free."

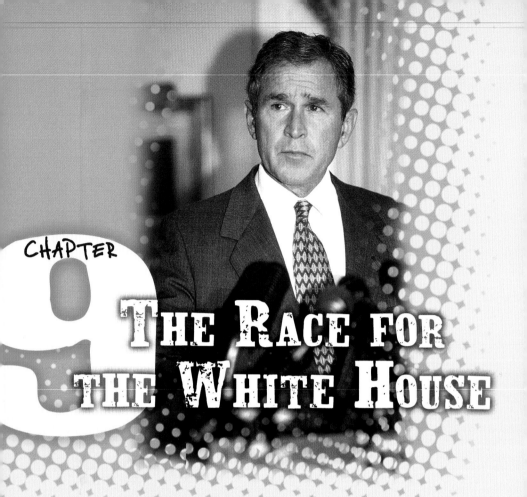

THE RACE FOR THE WHITE HOUSE

George W. decided to run for president in 1998. He knew he would have a long, hard campaign ahead of him.

GEORGE W. BUSH'S RACE for the White House began in 1998. After almost eight years of President Bill Clinton, a Democrat, many people were tired of having a Democrat in the White House.

Bush was sure he wanted to be president. But he wasn't sure if he wanted to run for president. Campaigns, especially presidential campaigns, get personal and nasty. He was worried about how hard a campaign would be on his teenaged twin daughters. He didn't want them to see people making fun of their father on *Saturday Night Live* or other television shows. And he knew he himself would miss his comfortable life. He liked to take long jogs and bounce around his Texas ranch in his Ford Explorer vehicle.

IT'S A FACT!

Political leaders are regularly spoofed on *Saturday Night Live.* The actor Will Ferrell has pretended to be George Bush on the show. (More recently, Chris Parnell has taken on this role.)

BETTING ON BUSH

In April 1998, Bush attended a private meeting at Stanford University in Palo Alto, California. Leading Republican thinkers wanted to meet Bush to see if he had what it takes to be president. They asked him questions about taxes, foreign policy, Social Security, terrorism, and other issues. Bush was understandably nervous. He realized that in many ways he was auditioning for the group. He realized that his future might depend on his performance. After many hours of questioning, Bush passed the test. The group thought he was pleasant, intelligent, and asked good questions. Bush himself seemed surprised at how well the meeting had gone. As he left the meeting, he joked that the group "didn't seem to think I was slobbering on my shoes."

Soon Republican leaders from around the country were making their way to Austin, Texas. They wanted to meet Bush for themselves. They brought their good wishes and money for his campaign. In June 1999, Bush formally announced that he would run for president. By then, he had raised more than $15 million to spend on the primary election. Eventually, he and national Republicans raised more than $350 million for the 2000 presidential election.

Bush and the Republican Party believed they would need every penny of it to win. The country was at peace. The economy was going well. The likely opponent was Vice President Al Gore, who had much more government and campaign experience than Bush did. The Republicans' big hope was that Gore would make a huge mistake, which wasn't likely.

ELECTION BATTLES

Before Bush could campaign against Gore, he had to win the Republican primary election. He faced a tough opponent in Senator John McCain of Arizona, a former Vietnam War hero. In the first primary, held in New Hampshire on February 1, 2000, Bush lost to McCain. But Bush defeated McCain in the next primary, in South Carolina. By the end of March, Bush was clearly in the lead. The road was open for him to be the

Senator John McCain was one of George W.'s leading opponents for the Republican nomination in 2000.

Republican candidate for president. He accepted the nomination during the Republican National Convention in Philadelphia in July. His teary-eyed parents looked on. Laura Bush confidently gave the opening speech of the convention.

Once Bush had won the Republican primary, he got ready to face Al Gore in the November general election. The news media questioned Bush's intelligence, his lack of experience, and his casual attitude. Reporters started writing about how Bush seemed to smirk, as if he was always joking. Most of all, people wondered whether Bush was mature enough to be

George W. was named the Republican Party's presidential candidate. His informal, joking manner often drew negative media attention.

president. Al Gore was very intelligent and serious. He was, in some ways, the complete opposite of the fun-loving Bush.

And Bush didn't help himself by refusing to talk about what he called his wild youth. At one point, he told a reporter he wasn't going to talk about what he'd done thirty years in the past. "I famously, and perhaps foolishly, said, 'When I was young and irresponsible, I sometimes behaved young and irresponsibly,'" Bush said. He said that he thought that was a funny way to say he was not perfect. But many people did not think it was funny. They wanted Bush to give private details about his younger days.

Luckily, Bush had plenty of smart people around him giving him advice. He picked Dick Cheney as his vice-presidential running mate. Cheney was a former congressman from Wyoming. He had served as the elder Bush's secretary of defense during his presidency. Voters knew that he had plenty of experience dealing with serious matters. But picking a member of his father's government for his vice president caused Bush some trouble. People wondered how much George W. had gained from his father's name and accomplishments. Bush responded to these people by saying he was very proud of his father but that he was his own man.

Bush also had to prove to voters that he was smart enough to be president. He had to make sure he didn't do or say anything outrageous. People laughed at Bush when he called the citizens of Greece "Grecians" instead of Greeks. At one campaign stop, he asked the crowd, "Is our children learning?" Another time he was overheard calling a reporter for the *New York Times* a vulgar name. Many people poked fun at Bush for these mishaps.

IT'S A FACT!

Poking fun at Bush's misspeaks was a favorite game for many people during the 2000 election. They named his mistakes Bushisms.

Television comedians like David Letterman, Jay Leno, and the players on *Saturday Night Live* made jokes about the candidates. This was the first election in U.S. history where voters seemed to take comedians seriously in making decisions about the candidates. In fact, people were paying so much attention to the humor that both Bush and Gore found it necessary to appear on some of the

George W.'s ability to relax and laugh was useful during an appearance on Oprah Winfrey's television show.

television comedy shows. They needed to prove that they could take a joke.

FINAL CAMPAIGN PUSH

As the November election neared, Bush faced one final tough test: candidate debates. In debates, candidates appear together to respond to questions from journalists or citizens. Many of the questions are about the candidates' plans as president. But they also include personal questions about how they feel on certain topics. Many people thought Bush would not do well in the debates. They thought Americans might not like his casual attitude, and they thought he might not seem as smart as Gore. Gore was considered to be one of the best debaters in the country. He could remember facts and was not afraid to attack an opponent. Newspaper reporters began to say that if Bush lost the debates or appeared to be ignorant, he would lose the election.

But to the surprise of many, Bush held his own against Gore. Bush was seen as a nice man who knew enough. He seemed relaxed, cheerful, friendly, and hopeful about the future. Bush survived the debates by not arguing with Gore and by constantly repeating his message over and over again. After holding his own in the debates, it seemed that Bush had a good chance of becoming the next president.

But just days before the election, some surprise news seemed like it would kill Bush's chances. The media reported that, as a young man, Bush had been

George W. (left) and Al Gore (right) appeared on TV debates in late 2000.

arrested for driving while intoxicated (DWI). Bush explained that he had not said anything about the arrest because he did not want his daughters to know about it. For a few days, people all across the country were talking about the news. Luckily, by the day before the election, it seemed that most voters had decided Bush's arrest should not keep him from being president.

No President . . . Yet

On November 7, 2000, millions of Americans cast their votes for their next president. That night and into the next morning, many stayed glued to the television as the results from each state were announced. But the matter of who would be president was not settled that night. It was not settled until thirty-five days after the vote. At the center of the delay was the state of Florida. A final decision in Florida couldn't be made because of problems with counting the votes. Whoever won in Florida would win the election. At first, the media declared that Gore had won the state. Then it appeared that Bush had won. In the days that followed, the Democratic and Republican parties asked the courts to settle the disagreement.

CHADS

The largest disagreement during the 2000 election was about Florida's voting system. Florida's system used punch cards as ballots. The cards only read a voter's choice after a section of the card's paper has been fully punched out next to the candidate's name. The punched-out part is called a "chad." For a vote to count in the counting machine, the chad must be completely removed.

The counter sends a beam of light toward the voting card. If the beam passes through a hole in the card, then the vote is recorded for the candidate. If the voter didn't punch completely through the ballot, the chad could still be attached. The "hanging chad" often blocks the hole and prevents the counting machine from reading the vote. Ballots with hanging chads were rejected, so no vote was counted.

The 2000 election between Bush and Gore was very close. For once, every vote seemed to count. Many Democrats said that Florida's rejected ballots could decide the election. Democrats and Republicans asked the Florida Supreme Court to help figure things out. Republicans told the court that if the counting machine couldn't find the vote, then the vote shouldn't be counted. Democrats told the court that every vote, even the unreadable ballots, should be looked at to figure out the winner.

The Florida count had a large number of unreadable punch cards. Judges looked at each one to tell for whom the voter was trying to vote. Many judges felt that if the punch card showed a vote, it should be counted. With each recount, Democratic presidential nominee Al Gore was slowly gaining ground. He might win the election. But then the recounting process hit several roadblocks. The outcome of the election was delayed again and again.

Finally, on December 13, 2000, Al Gore called Governor Bush. The U.S. Supreme Court had ordered the counting to stop, and Gore told Bush he believed he'd lost the presidential race. Bush was to be the president.

First, the Florida Supreme Court said they would ask Florida officials to recount the votes—a move that would probably help Gore. Then the U.S. Supreme Court ordered the counting to stop. This left Bush ahead by a few hundred votes. George W. Bush had finally secured his place in history. He would be the forty-third president of the United States.

But even after Bush was declared the winner, it seemed possible that he might not get to be president. It was possible that Congress could question his victory. Gore finally calmed the tense situation by appearing on television. He announced that he accepted the Court's decision, making Bush the next president, and he asked all Americans to support the new president. In response, Bush promised to be president to everyone in the United States and to unite the deeply divided country.

CHAPTER

10

PRESIDENT BUSH

George W. takes the oath of office in 2001 to become the forty-third U.S. president.

A FREEZING RAIN FELL on Washington, D.C., on January 20, 2001, as George W. Bush was sworn in as the forty-third president of the United States. But the unusual circumstances of the election left a cloud hanging over his victory. Many Americans were angry with the way the election had turned out. They felt that in Florida, every citizen's vote had not been counted. During the campaign, Bush had promised the country that he would be a

uniter and not a divider. Once he took the oath of
office, he had to make good on that promise by
giving the most important speech of his life.

To prepare, Bush had
spent five weeks reading
the inauguration speeches
of former presidents. He
knew that "he must use
this speech to wipe away,
like spilled milk, the
questions of the legitimacy
arising from his strange
path to the Oval Office."

In his speech, he
talked about one united
America. As millions
watched on television and
hundreds of friends and
family stood nearby, Bush
made a solemn pledge to
"work to build a single

IT'S A FACT!

George W. Bush's
election was only the
second time the son
of a former president
was elected to the
nation's highest
office. John Quincy
Adams, the son of
Founding Father
John Adams, had
become the nation's
sixth president in
1825. Aware of this,
Big George began
calling his son
Quincy.

nation of justice and opportunity. I know this is
within our reach." After Bush finished his speech,
supporters cheered on the Capitol steps. A band
began playing the traditional song reserved only

for the president of the United States, "Hail to the Chief."

Even as the music was playing, however, thousands of protesters chanted and yelled in the streets of Washington, D.C. Police officers stood every few feet along the route of the inauguration parade. The protesters claimed that Bush had been selected (by the Supreme Court) and not elected to the presidency. One sign in the crowd said, "Hail to the Thief."

George W.'s inauguration did not end protests. Many people didn't support the election results.

DOWN TO BUSINESS

President George W. Bush was determined not to let the election controversy get in the way of his plans for the country. During his first meeting with leaders from Congress, he said, "Expectations in this country [are] we can't get anything done. [People are saying,] 'Well, gosh, the election was so close, nothing will happen except finger-pointing and name-calling and bitterness.' I'm here to tell the country that things will get done, that we're going to rise above expectations, that both Republicans and Democrats will come together to do what's right for America."

With those words, Bush began his presidency. Both houses of Congress–the Senate and the House of Representatives–had about the same number of Republicans and Democrats. This made it hard for the new president to get many new laws passed during his first few months. But the government did write and pass one major new law during early 2001. A new tax law changed the way taxes were paid and made changes to older Americans' retirement savings plans.

ATTACK ON THE UNITED STATES

On September 11, 2001 (9/11), tragedy struck the United States. Terrorists hijacked four U.S. passenger airplanes and used them as weapons against the American people. They flew two of the planes into the towers of the World Trade Center in New York City and a third plane into the Pentagon near Washington, D.C. These buildings were symbols of U.S. business and military power. A

George W. Bush greets firefighters and rescue workers. He was at the site the day after terrorists crashed a hijacked passenger plane into the headquarters of the U.S. Department of Defense located in the Pentagon in Washington, D.C.

fourth plane did not make its target and crashed in
the Pennsylvania countryside. Thousands of people
lost their lives in the attacks.

The night of September 11, President Bush
spoke to grief-stricken, terrified Americans. "These
acts shattered steel, but they cannot dent the steel
of American resolve," he said. Within weeks, the
U.S. government declared that they had evidence
that a terrorist group called al-Qaeda was
responsible for the terrorist attacks. Al-Qaeda was
based in Afghanistan and is headed by a man
named Osama bin Laden.

Bush announced to the nation that the United
States was involved in a new kind of war: a war on

OSAMA BIN LADEN

The U.S. government was familiar with Osama bin Laden before 9/11.
Many agencies had been tracking the al-Qaeda leader since his members
had tried to blow up the World Trade Center in 1993. But things had
been quiet. Just before 9/11, people were still discussing whether or not
bin Laden and his organization were dangerous to the United States.

As of mid-2005, Osama bin Laden has yet to be found, and many wonder
if the al-Qaeda leader is still alive. Audio and video recordings of bin
Laden are often aired on television. The date of these recordings is hard
to determine. So experts are brought in to decide if the recordings are
real. U.S. officials hope this information will help them find bin Laden.

terrorism. The U.S. military gained approval to attack terrorist leaders hiding in Afghanistan. They destroyed training facilities and bases of al-Qaeda but were not able to find bin Laden. The United States soon discovered that al-Qaeda was spread out all over the world. Bush was determined to fight terrorists wherever they lived. He told the American public that this was an unusual kind of war, with no clear end in sight. "The only way to defeat terrorism as a threat to our way of life is to stop it, eliminate it and destroy it where it grows," he said. He placed the war on terrorism at the top of his list of priorities for the United States.

WAR IN IRAQ

Meanwhile, in 2002, the Bush administration said that they had discovered proof of weapons of mass destruction (WMDs) in the country of Iraq. WMDs include nuclear, biological, and any other weapons that can quickly wipe out large areas of the world. Bush's government said it had photographs of these types of weapons being made in Iraq. Bush told Americans that Iraq's leader, Saddam Hussein, was a threat to the world and to his own people. Bush tried to get approval from the United Nations to invade Iraq. When the United Nations did not agree to the invasion, Bush asked Congress to approve an invasion of Iraq. He said the United States had to attack Iraq in order to remove Saddam Hussein from power and to keep the world safe. Congress voted to allow the U.S. military to invade Iraq. The Iraq war, known as "Operation Iraqi Freedom," began in March 2003.

IT'S A FACT!

Officially, the United Nations did not support the war in Iraq. Both France and Germany stopped a war resolution from passing. Both countries wanted to give weapons inspectors more time to find WMDs.

Many people in the United States and the rest of the world were deeply upset that the U.S. military had attacked Iraq. They pointed out that Iraq had never attacked the United States or even threatened to. They also felt that the Iraq war would take away energy and money needed to find Osama bin Laden and the others responsible for the 9/11 attacks.

In April 2003, U.S troops overtook the Iraqi capital city of Baghdad. Saddam Hussein went into hiding. On May 2, 2003, President Bush stood on

On May 2, 2003, aboard the USS *Abraham Lincoln,* Bush declared the U.S.-led mission to be accomplished.

board the flight deck of the USS *Abraham Lincoln* in front of a huge banner that read "Mission Accomplished." Bush declared that "major combat operations in Iraq have ended." But many Americans were angry at the president's statement, since many U.S. troops were still fighting and dying in Iraq.

Later that year, the president made a surprise visit to Iraq to share Thanksgiving dinner with the troops. He spent two hours eating with soldiers in the Baghdad airport. The visit was kept top secret, and even the troops had no idea he was coming. A few weeks later, on December 13, U.S. military agents captured Saddam Hussein. This event was a great achievement for President Bush. Most Americans–even those who disagreed with the president about the war in Iraq–were glad that Hussein had been taken.

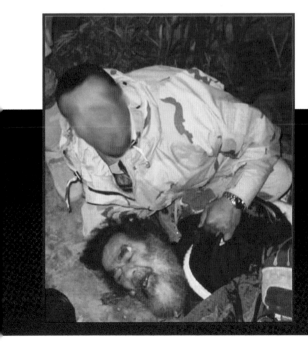

U. S. soldiers captured Saddam Hussein (bottom) on December 13, 2003.

ELECTION 2004

By the spring of 2004, no WMDs had been found in Iraq. In fact, the proof that Bush had relied on turned out to be inaccurate. In May of 2004, only 46 percent of Americans said they approved of the president. Some said that the president had lied about the WMDs in order to get control of Iraq's valuable oil. They said that Bush had sent young Americans to fight and die in Iraq for financial gain.

The father of two sons serving in Iraq holds up a protest sign. Military families and veterans gathered in Washington, D.C., to call for the end of the U.S. occupation of Iraq.

U.S. military medical staff in Iraq are wearing gear to protect them from WMDs.

Others felt that the president had good reason to attack Iraq. They believed that WMDs really did exist in that country and that Bush was acting in the best interest of the United States. These disagreements divided Americans in the months before the 2004 presidential election.

By the summer of 2004, Americans were deeply divided in their opinions about President Bush. They either wanted to vote him out of office, or they felt he was one of the great leaders of history. Many voters were still angry about the way Bush had become president in 2000. These strong feelings led to a huge interest in politics during the 2004 election.

Hip-hop artist Sean Combs attended a voter rally at MTV Studios on November 2, 2004. He challenged young people to vote.

Bush's Democratic opponent was a Vietnam War hero, Senator John Kerry of Massachusetts. Kerry told Americans that the president had led them, with false information, into an unnecessary war in Iraq. Meanwhile, he said, Bush had not paid enough attention to finding Osama bin Laden or to issues such as jobs and health care in the United States. The campaign battles between Bush and Kerry were harsh. Many groups got involved on both sides to try to get new voters to vote in this important election.

Many people worried about a repeat of the 2000 election. They thought it might be several weeks—or even months—after the election before Americans would know who their next president would be. But by early on the morning after Election Day, November 2, 2004, Bush was declared the winner, fair and square, with 51 percent of the votes. More than 59 million American voters had chosen George W. Bush to lead the country for four more years.

GLOSSARY

Civil Rights Act: a law that made segregation (having separate black facilities and white facilities) illegal in public places, such as parks, libraries, and restaurants. President Lyndon Johnson signed the law in 1964.

Democratic Party: one of the two major political parties of the United States. The Republican Party, Bush's party, is the other.

foreign policy: a nation's dealings with other countries. These dealings can include such things as treaties and trade agreements.

leukemia: a form of cancer that attacks the blood and the blood cells

National Guard: a state-run reserve military unit. Each state recruits its own National Guard, and the U.S. government pays for equipment.

al-Qaeda: a terrorist group founded in about 1989. It is headed by Osama bin Laden.

Republican Party: one of the two major political parties in the United States. Bush belongs to the Republican Party. The other major party is the Democratic Party.

Social Security: a U.S. government program that gives money, health care, and other benefits to workers at retirement

stock: a share, or part ownership, of a company

United Nations: an international organization founded in 1945 to solve problems among nations. Most nations of the world are members of the United Nations.

U.S. Supreme Court: the highest court in the United States. Decisions made by judges on the U.S. Supreme Court affect the entire country.

Vietnam War: a conflict that took place from 1957 to 1975 in the present-day Southeast Asian nation of Vietnam. The United States was involved from the 1960s through 1975.

weapon of mass destruction (WMD): a weapon that can kill or hurt a huge number of people at once

welfare system: a large group of services and benefits that the U.S. government pays for to help poor, unemployed, and other people

SOURCE NOTES

14 George Lardner Jr. and Lois Romano, "Tragedy Created Bush Mother-Son Bond," *Washington Post*, July 26, 1999, A-1.

15 Ibid.

15-16 George W. Bush, *A Charge to Keep* (New York: William Morrow and Company, Inc., 1999), 14.

16 Elizabeth Mitchell, *W: Revenge of the Bush Dynasty* (New York: Hyperion, 2000), 34.

16 Ibid.

18 Bush, 20.

18 Ibid., 19.

18-19 Ibid.

21-22 George Lardner Jr. and Lois Romano, "Bush: So-So Student but a Campus Mover," *Washington Post*, July 27, 1999, A-1.

28 "DKE History," *DKE Headquarters*, n.d., http://www.dke.org/history.html (May 12, 2005).

29 "Bush: So-So Student," A-1.

29 Bush, 47.

38-39 Ibid., 50-51

49 George Lardner Jr. and Lois Romano, "At Height of Vietnam, Bush Picks Guard," *Washington Post*, July 28, 1999, A-1.

49 Bush, 59.

50 Ibid.

50 "At Height of Vietnam, Bush Picks Guard," A-1.

50 Bush, 59

60 George Lardner Jr. and Lois Romano, "Bush Name Helps Fuel Oil Dealings," *Washington Post*, July 30, 1999, A-1.

61 Daniel Cohen, *George W. Bush: The Family Business* (Brookfield, CT: The Millbrook Press, 2000), 25.

65 Bush, 132-33.

72 J.H. Hatfield, *Fortunate Son: George W. Bush and the Making of an American President* (New York: Soft Skull Press, 2000), 119.

73-74 Cohen, 30.

74 Hatfield, 124.

75 George Lardner Jr. and Lois Romano, "Bush's Move up to the Majors," *Washington Post*, July 31, 1999, A-1.

77 Ibid.

80 Evan Thomas et al., "The Favorite Son: Pumping Iron, Digging Gold, Pressing Flesh," *Newsweek*, November 20, 2000, 51.

83 Bush, 133.

84 Ronald Kessler, *A Matter of Character: Inside the White House of George W. Bush*, (New York : Sentinel, 2004), 127.

91 David E. Sanger, "Momentous Challenges as Bush Reaches for 12 Minutes of Inaugural Fame," *New York Times*, n.d., http://www.nytimes.com (January 20, 2001).

91 Melinda Henneberger, "The Inauguration: The Speech; In His Address, Bush Lingers on a Promise to Care," *New York Times*, January 21, 2001, 13.

93 Nick Anderson, James Gerstenzang, and Doyle

McManus, "Bush Vows to Bring Nation Together," *Los Angeles Times*, January 21, 2001, http://www.latimes.com (n.d.).

95 "Bush Condemns Attacks, Vows to 'find those responsible,' " *Startribune.com*, September 12, 2001, http://www.startribune .com/stories/484/685011.html (September 17, 2001).

96 "Address to a Joint Session of Congress and the American People," *The White House*, September 20, 2001, http://www.whitehouse.gov/ne ws/releases/2001/09/20010920-8.html (May 12, 2005).

98 "President Bush Announces Major Combat Operations in Iraq Have Ended," *The White House*, May 1, 2003, http://www.whitehouse.gov/ne ws/releases/2003/05/iraq/2003 0501-15.html (May 12, 2005).

SELECTED BIBLIOGRAPHY

Anderson, Nick, James Gerstenzang, and Doyle McManus. "Bush Vows to Bring Nation Together." *Los Angeles Times*, January 21, 2001, http://www.latimes.com (n.d.).

Bush, George W. *A Charge to Keep*. New York: William Morrow and Company, Inc., 1999.

Cohen, Daniel. *George W. Bush: The Family Business*. Brookfield, CT: The Millbrook Press, 2000.

Fineman, Howard, and Martha Brant. "The Test of His Life." *Newsweek*, December 25, 2000/January 1, 2001.

Hatfield, J. H. *Fortunate Son: George W. Bush and the Making of an American President*. New York: Soft Skull Press, 2000.

Ivins, Molly, and Lou Dubose. *Shrub: The Short but Happy Political Life of George W. Bush*. New York: Random House, 2000.

Kakutani, Michiko. "An Essay: With the Guy Next Door in the Oval Office, the Presidency Shrinks Further." *New York Times*, January 19, 2001. http://www.nytimes.com (January 26, 2001).

Mitchell, Elizabeth. *W: Revenge of the Bush Dynasty*. New York: Hyperion, 2000.

Sanger, David E. "Momentous Challenges as Bush Reaches for 12 Minutes of Inaugural Fame." *New York Times*, N.d. http://www.nytimes.com (January 20, 2001).

Sheehy, Gail. "The Accidental Candidate." *Vanity Fair*, October 2000.

Thomas, Evan, et al. "The Favorite Son: Pumping Iron, Digging Gold, Pressing Flesh." *Newsweek*, November 20, 2000.

FURTHER READING AND WEBSITES

Burgan, Michael. *George W. Bush: Our Forty-Third President.* Chanhassen, MN: Child's World, 2005.

Democratic National Committee (DNC)
www.democrats.org
This site is dedicated to the Democratic Party. It includes historical information about the DNC as well as information about its leaders. Also included in the site are press releases, a merchandise store, and resources for people interested in joining the Democratic Party.

Donnelly, Matt. *George W. Bush: America's 43rd President.* Danbury, CT: Children's Press, 2005.

Gormley, Beatrice. *Laura Bush: America's First Lady.* New York: Aladdin Paperbacks, 2003.

Gormley, Beatrice. *President George W. Bush: Our Forty-Third President.* New York: Aladdin Paperbacks, 2001.

Hughes, Libby. *George W. Bush: From Texas to the White House.* New York: Franklin Watts, 2003.

Kachurek, Sandra J. *George W. Bush.* Berkeley Heights, NJ: Enslow Publishers, 2004.

Marsh, Carole, and Kathy Zimmer. *George W. Bush: America's Newest President, and His White House Family.* The Here & Now Series. Peachtree City, GA: Gallopade International, 2001.

McNeese, Tim. *George W. Bush: First President of the New Century.* Greensboro, N.C.: Morgan Reynolds Publishing, 2002.

Republican National Committee
www.gop.org
This site is dedicated to the Republican Party. It includes information about Republican party leaders, history, recent news articles, and even the official store.

Russell, Jon, ed. *The Complete Book of Inaugural Addresses of the Presidents of the United States: From George Washington to George W. Bush 1789 to 2001.* Seattle: iUniverse Online Books, 2001.

Schuman, Michael. *George H.W. Bush.* Berkeley Heights, NJ: Enslow Publishers, 2002.

Sergis, Diana. *Bush V. Gore: Controversial Presidential Election Case.* Berkeley Heights, NJ: Enslow Publishers, 2003.

Stone, Tanya Lee. *Laura Welch Bush: First Lady.* Brookfield, CT: Millbrook Press, 2001.

The White House
http://www.whitehouse.gov/president/gwbbio.html
The official White House biography of President George W. Bush offers a brief description of his life and career. The site includes speeches and statements made by the president on a number of topics and also contains links to other government sites and biographies.

PHOTO ACKNOWLEDGMENTS

Photographs were used with the permission of: © Reuters NewMedia
Inc./CORBIS, pp. 4, 5, 82, 92; © Reuters/CORBIS, p. 7; © Joseph Sohm;
ChromoSohm Inc./CORBIS, pp. 8 (left), 81; © Lisa O'Connor/ZUMA Press,
p. 8 (right); George Bush Presidential Library, pp. 10, 11, 15, 24, 27, 39, 55, 56,
59, 63; Classmates.com Yearbook Archives, pp. 20, 21; © Rykoff
Collection/CORBIS, p. 33; National Archives, p. 35; Independent Picture
Service, p. 36 (left); Office of the Senator, p. 36 (right); © AFP/Getty Images,
p. 42; © Bettmann/ CORBIS, pp. 45, 65, 69; © Wally McNamee/CORBIS,
p. 53; Carol T. Powers, The White House, p. 70; David Woo/The Dallas
Morning News, p. 73; AP/Wide World Photos, pp. 77, 85, 90; © Jana
Birchman, p. 78; © Henry Ray Abrams/AFP/Getty Images, p. 86; © Paul J.
Richards/AFP/Getty Images, p. 94; © Stephen JAFFE/AFP/Getty Images, p.
98; © PPS Vienna/ZUMA Press, p. 99; © Mark Wilson/Getty Images, p. 100;
Defense Visual Information Center (DVIC), p. 101; © Nancy Kaszerman/
ZUMA Press, p. 102.
Cover: Eric Draper, White House/United States Department of Defense.